SCHIRMER'S LIBRARY
OF MUSICAL CLASSICS

Vol. 2141

J.S. BACH:
EASIEST PIANO PIECES

38 Pieces from the English Suites, French Suites, Inventions, Well-Tempered Clavier, and more

ISBN 978-1-5400-4180-7

G. SCHIRMER, Inc.

DISTRIBUTED BY

7777 W. BLUEMOUND RD. P.O. BOX 13819 MILWAUKEE, WI 53213

www.schirmer.com
www.halleonard.com

CONTENTS

SARABANDE
from English Suite No. 2 in A minor

Johann Sebastian Bach
BWV 807

The ornaments (agréments) of the same Sarabande.

GAVOTTE I and II

from English Suite No. 3 in G minor

Johann Sebastian Bach
BWV 808

Gavotte I (alternatively)
Molto Allegro (♩=100)

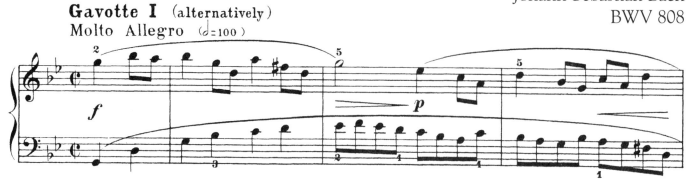

Gavotte II (or the Musette)
L'istesso tempo

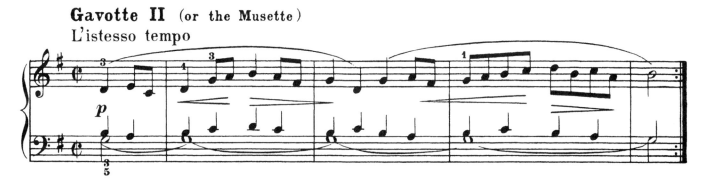

Gavotte I Da Capo

MENUET I and II

from English Suite No. 4 in F Major

Johann Sebastian Bach
BWV 809

Menuet I

Andante con moto (♩ = 116)

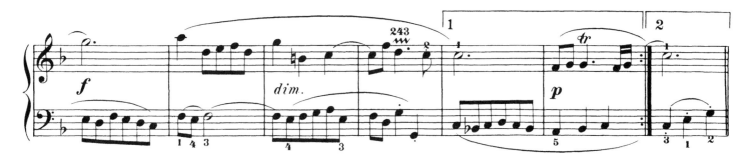

Menuet II

Menuet I D.C.

SARABANDE

from English Suite No. 5 in E minor

Johann Sebastian Bach

BWV 810

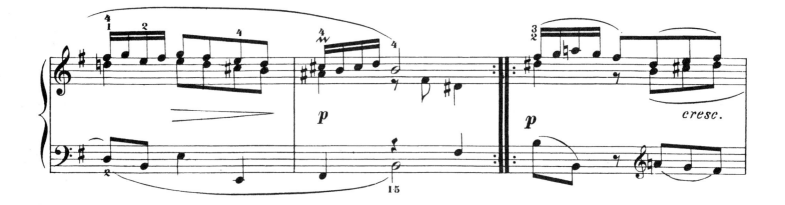

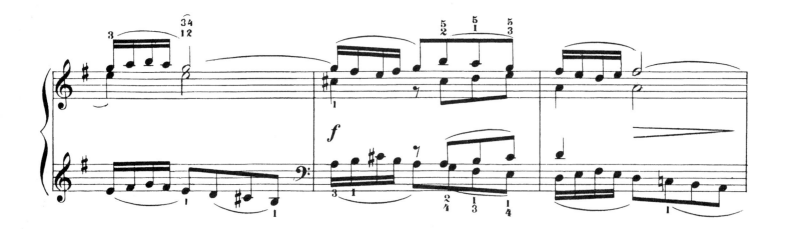

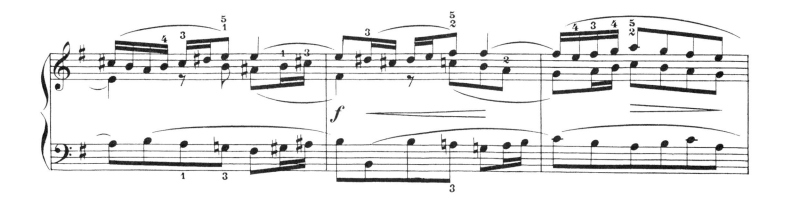

SARABANDE AND DOUBLE

from English Suite No. 6 in D minor

Johann Sebastian Bach

BWV 811

Sarabande

Andante con moto (♩=60)

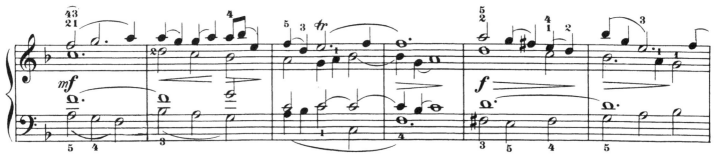

Double

GAVOTTE II

from English Suite No. 6 in D minor

Johann Sebastian Bach
BWV 811

SARABANDE

from French Suite No. 2 in C minor

Johann Sebastian Bach

BWV 813

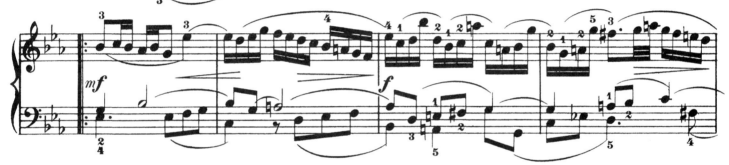

MENUET
from French Suite No. 2 in C minor

Johann Sebastian Bach
BWV 813

SARABANDE

from French Suite No. 4 in E-flat Major

Johann Sebastian Bach

BWV 815

MENUET
from French Suite No. 4 in E-flat Major

Johann Sebastian Bach
BWV 815

BOURRÉE
from French Suite No. 5 in G minor

Johann Sebastian Bach
BWV 816

GAVOTTE
from French Suite No. 5 in G minor

Johann Sebastian Bach
BWV 816

Gavotte
Un poco vivace ($\quad$ = 88)

GAVOTTE

from French Suite No. 6 in E Major

Johann Sebastian Bach
BWV 817

MENUET
from French Suite No. 6 in E Major

Johann Sebastian Bach
BWV 817

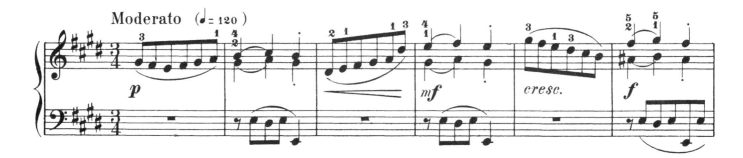

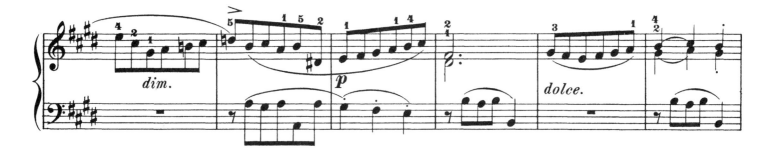

ARIA DA CAPO

in G Major
from *Goldberg Variations*

Johann Sebastian Bach
BWV 988

BOURÉE
from Lute Suite No. 1 in E minor

Johann Sebastian Bach
BWV 996

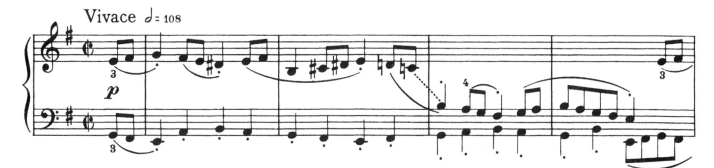

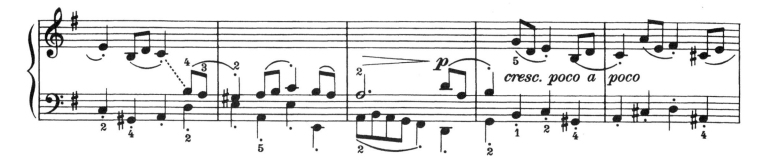

MENUET
from Overture in F Major

Johann Sebastian Bach
BWV 820

GAVOTTE
from Overture in G minor

Johann Sebastian Bach
BWV 822

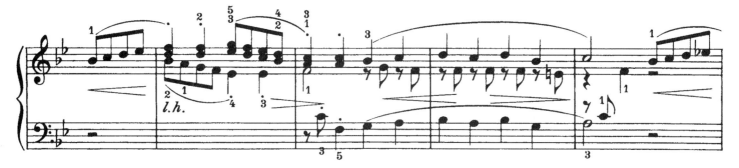

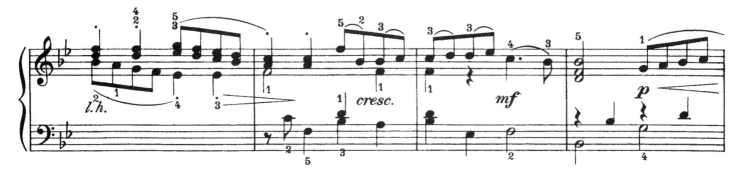

MENUET I
from Overture in G minor

Johann Sebastian Bach
BWV 822

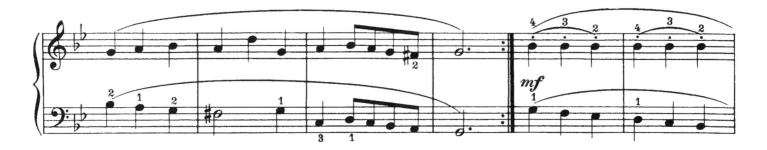

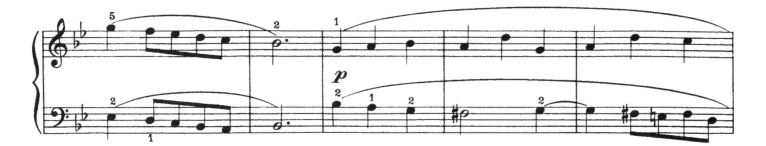

MENUET II

from Overture in G minor

Johann Sebastian Bach
BWV 822

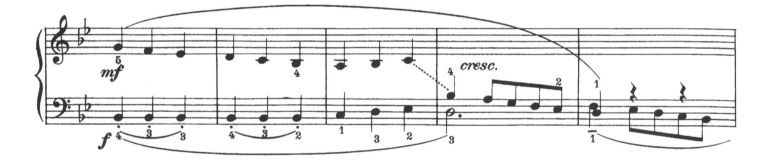

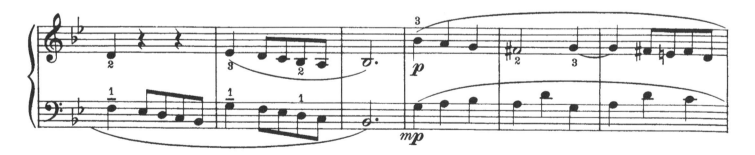

SARABANDE

from Partita No. 2 in C minor

Johann Sebastian Bach
BWV 826

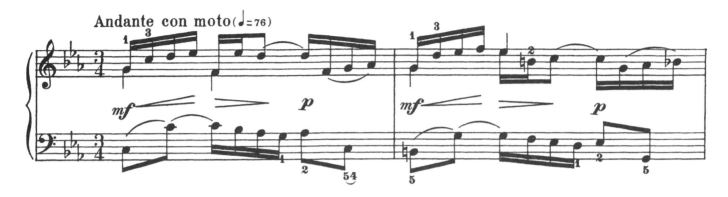

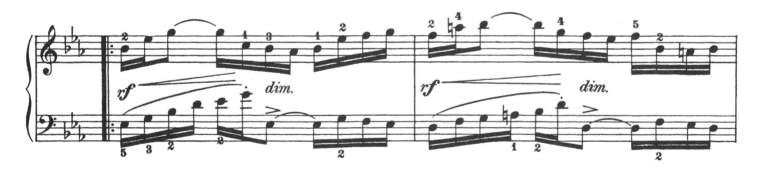

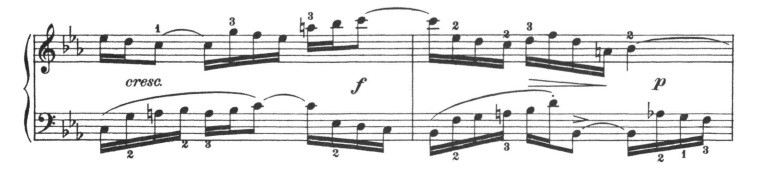

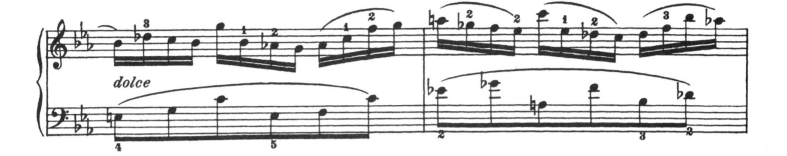

MENUET I and II

from Partita No. 1 in B-flat Major

Johann Sebastian Bach

BWV 825

Menuet I

Menuet II

PRELUDE
in C Major

Johann Sebastian Bach
BWV 924

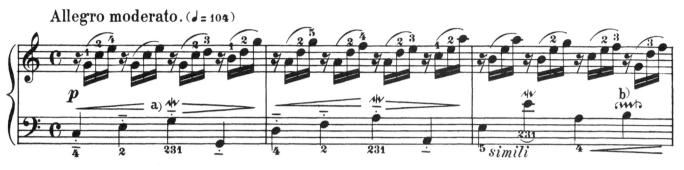

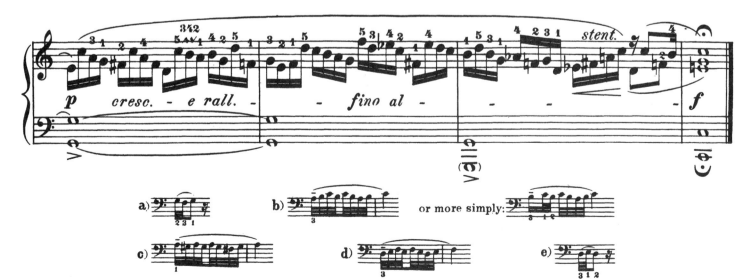

PRELUDE
in G Major

Johann Sebastian Bach
BWV 902a

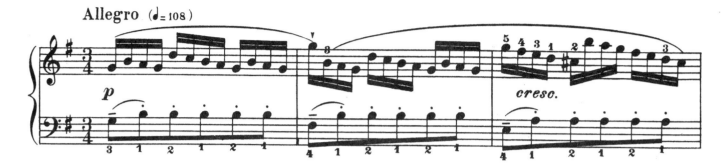

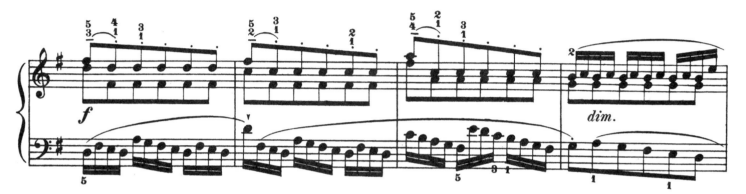

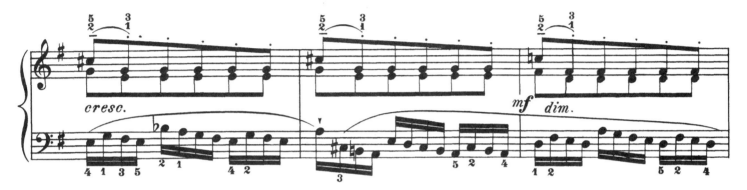

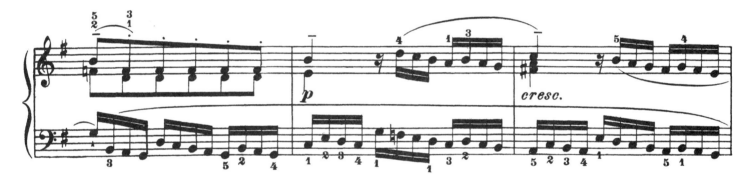

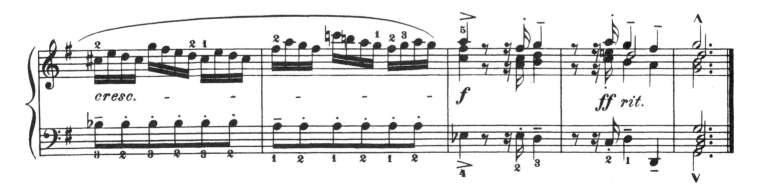

INVENTION NO. 1
in C Major

Johann Sebastian Bach
BWV 772

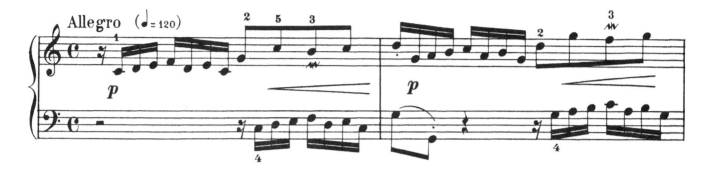

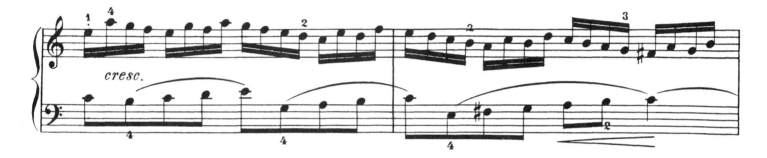

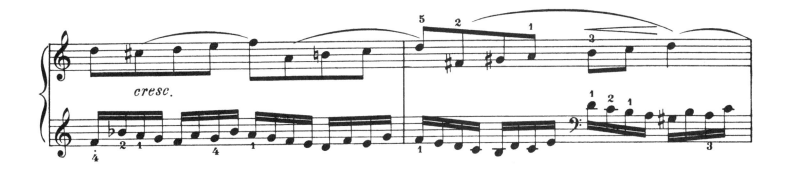

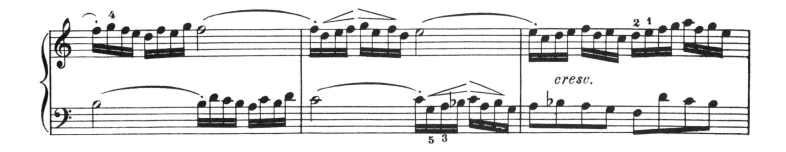

INVENTION NO. 2

in C minor

Johann Sebastian Bach
BWV 773

Allegro moderato (♩=108)

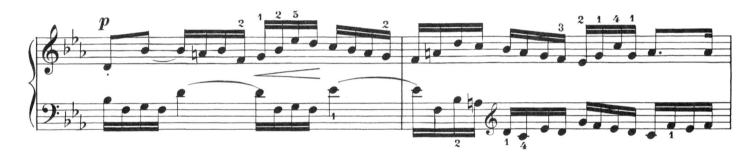

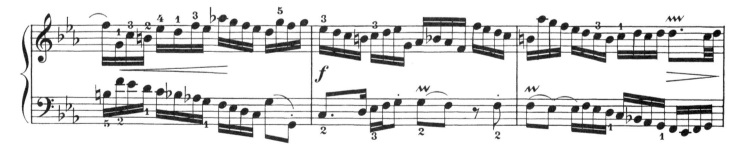

INVENTION NO. 4

in D minor

Johann Sebastian Bach

BWV 775

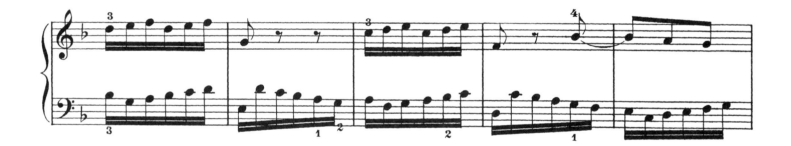

INVENTION NO. 14

in B-flat Major

Johann Sebastian Bach

BWV 785

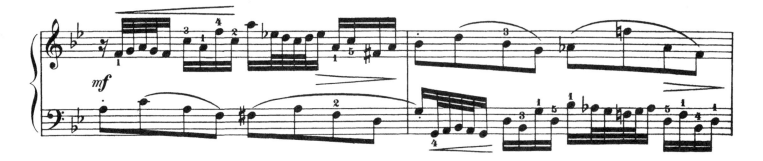

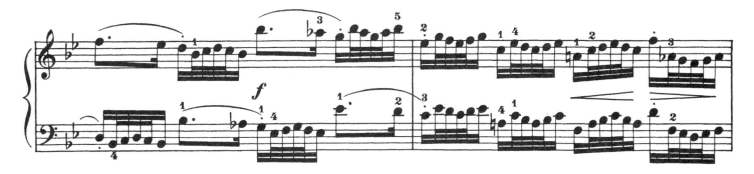

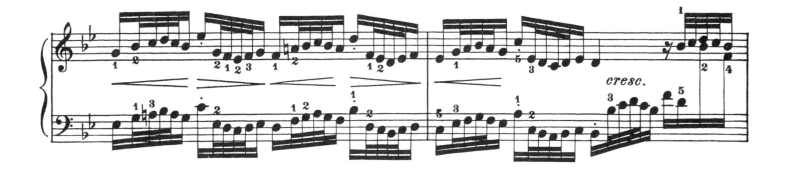

PRELUDE NO. 1

in C Major

from *The Well-Tempered Clavier*, Book I

Johann Sebastian Bach

BWV 846

PRELUDE NO. 9

in E Major

from *The Well-Tempered Clavier*, Book I

Johann Sebastian Bach

BWV 854

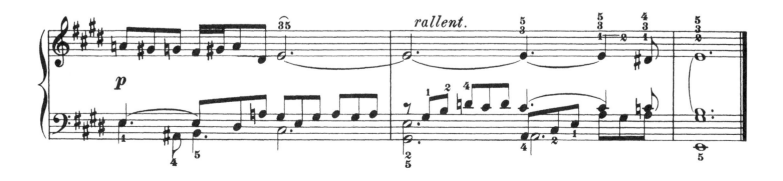

PRELUDE NO. 12

in F minor

from *The Well-Tempered Clavier*, Book I

Johann Sebastian Bach

BWV 857

Andante espressivo (♪ = 104)

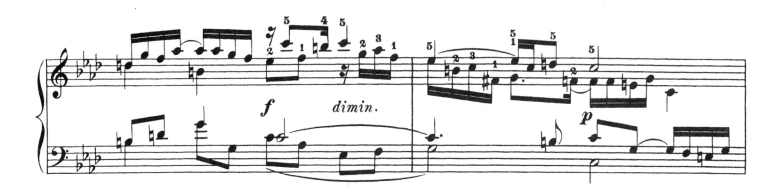

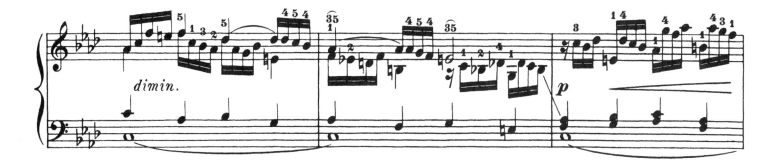

PRELUDE NO. 16

in G minor

from *The Well-Tempered Clavier*, Book I

Johann Sebastian Bach

BWV 861

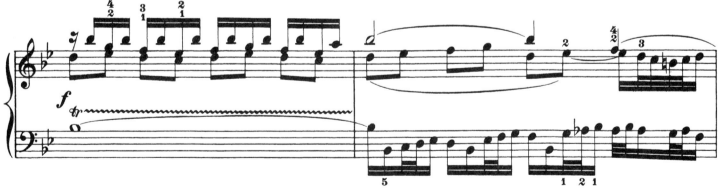

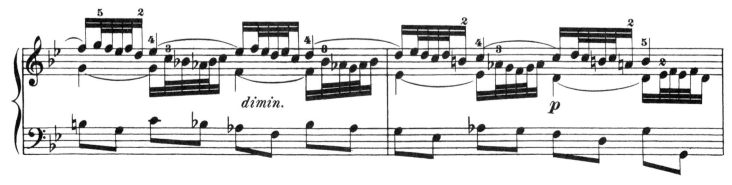

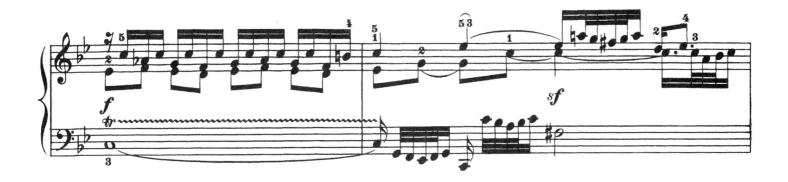

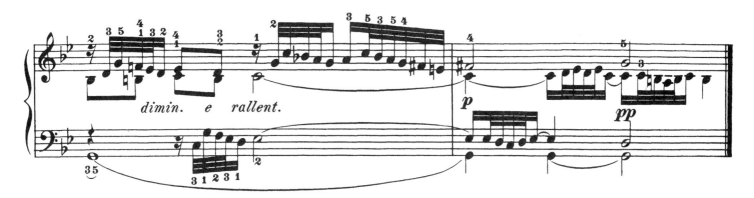

PRELUDE NO. 1

in C Major

from *The Well-Tempered Clavier*, Book II

Johann Sebastian Bach

BWV 870

PRELUDE NO. 7
in E-flat Major
from *The Well-Tempered Clavier*, Book II

Johann Sebastian Bach
BWV 876

Allegretto moderato (♩. = 84)

FUGUE NO. 7

in E-flat Major

from *The Well-Tempered Clavier*, Book II

Johann Sebastian Bach

BWV 876

FUGUE NO. 9

in E Major

from *The Well-Tempered Clavier*, Book II

Johann Sebastian Bach

BWV 878

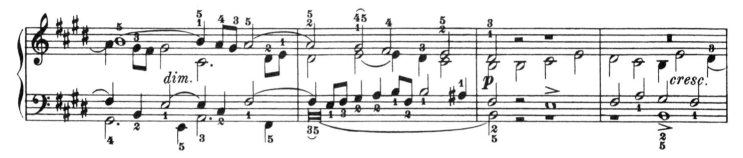

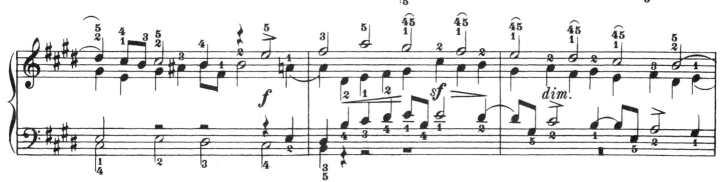

PRELUDE NO. 12
in F minor
from *The Well-Tempered Clavier*, Book II

Johann Sebastian Bach

BWV 881

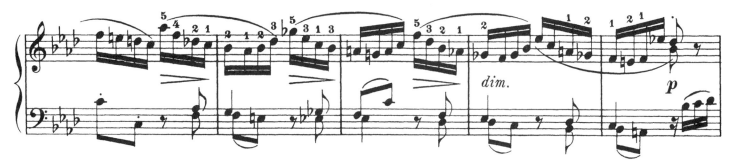

PRELUDE NO. 16

in G minor

from *The Well-Tempered Clavier*, Book II

Johann Sebastian Bach

BWV 885

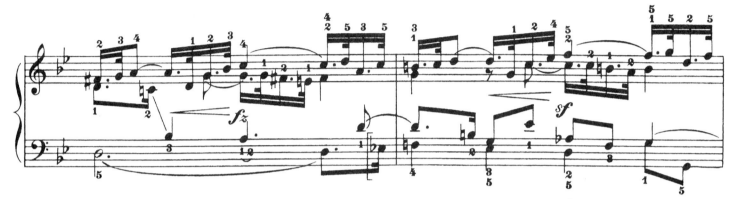

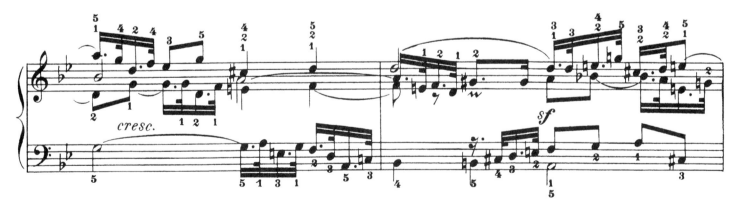

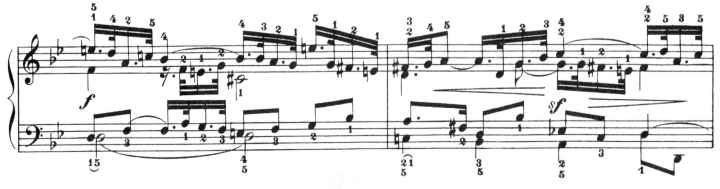

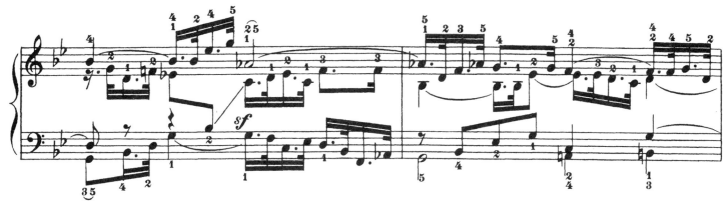

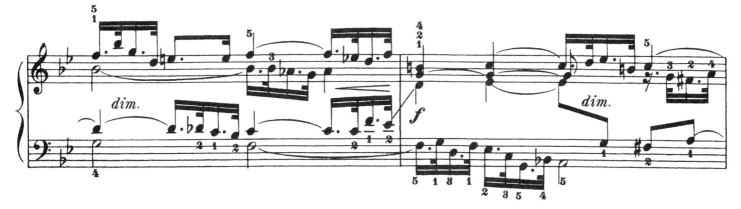

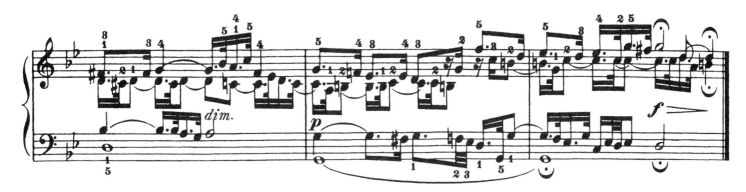

PRELUDE
in C Major

Johann Sebastian Bach
BWV 939

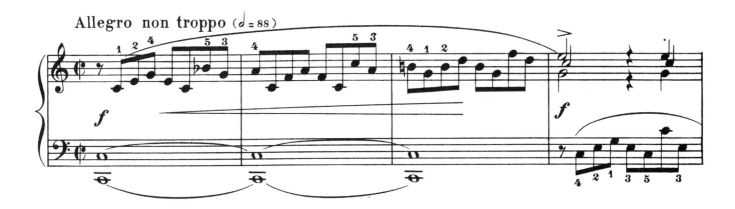

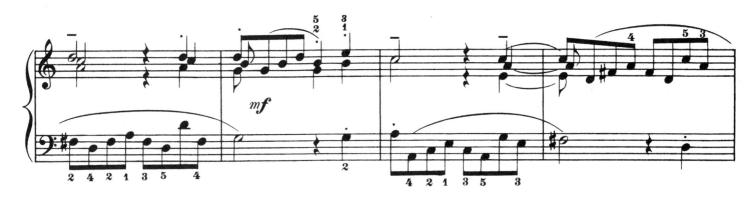